Making Sense of Peace

Making Sense of Peace

A Practical Guide to a Peaceful Life

Fritzroy E. Petty

Outskirts Press, Inc.
Denver, Colorado

Making Sense of Peace
A Practical Guide to a Peaceful Life
All Rights Reserved.
Copyright © 2011 Fritzroy E. Petty
v3.0

Cover Photo © 2011 JupiterImages Corporation. All rights reserved - used with permission.

Scripture quotations were taken from the *King James Version*.

Kingdom Crew Ministries
P.O. Box 308325
St. Thomas, VI 00803
340-774-1643 / fepetty@hotmail.com

Outskirts Press, Inc.
http://www.outskirtspress.com

ISBN: 978-1-4327-7573-5

Outskirts Press and the "OP" logo are trademarks belonging to Outskirts Press, Inc.

PRINTED IN THE UNITED STATES OF AMERICA

Acknowledgements

I would like to thank my family for the time they allowed me to complete this work. It took several years to accomplish the task, as simple as it may seem. My wife, Emily, and my children, Jamian and J'analise, were patient and encouraging. Emily, thanks for being there for me when I could not seemingly understand what I was going through. You never condemned me and were compassionate to my needs. May this book also help you as you navigate through life. Jamian and J'analise, as you grow I hope that this book will be a comfort to you when you are facing some of life's struggles. I love all of you with all my heart! I would also like to give special thanks to Larry and Enid Danet and all the family for listening to me when I expressed my experiences and helping me to make sense of the peace of God by your words of encouragement.

I am grateful for the help from Pastor James E. Petty, my brother and pastor, for encouraging me and reviewing this project. Elder Edwin Roland White, you have been my first pastor. Your discipline and support helped to form my early thinking, and you continue to be a source of wisdom. Apostle Vernon Eng, thank you for your valuable deposit in my spiritual development. You helped me to adjust the information in this book to be present-able to the audience. To all my immediate family, friends, and associates, I would like to say a heartfelt thank you. I hope that you are blessed from the words in this book.

Contents

Introduction ix

Chapter 1 1

The Battle of the Mind

Chapter 2 5

Faith vs. Emotions

Chapter 3 9

Faith vs. Fear

Chapter 4 15

Always Stay Focused on God!

Chapter 5 17

Get Busy and Stay Busy for God

Chapter 6 19

Forget Yesterday's Old Thoughts: "Celebrate Today!"

Chapter 7 25

The True Power of Peace

Chapter 8 27

Making Sense of Peace

Introduction

Making sense of peace may seem to make no sense if you feel perfectly sound. Why should you need to make sense of what you already have? What if I told you that there are battles going on right now for your right to have peace? For instance, in the United States, we enjoy freedom and peace in our respective states, territories, counties, towns, cities, etc. However, there are terrorists who are diligently at work trying to disrupt our peace and terrorize us. They are planning attacks against the United States as I am writing this book. At the same time, there are soldiers, special agents, and other Americans in Afghanistan and other parts of the world fighting the forces who intend us harm.

To understand this practical guide to making sense of peace, I need to explain some basic foundational truths. First, you must be aware that there is a spiritual world of beings that represent good and evil. The creator of this world is God himself. God, who consists of the Father, Son, and Holy Ghost (the trinity), created us in his image. We are body, soul, and spirit (I Thessalonians 5:23). In the book of Genesis, God described how he created Adam. Specifically, he formed him from the dust of the ground, breathed the breath of life into his nostrils, and he became a living soul. What is very important here is that he did not become conscious until God breathed the breath of life into his nostrils. There is no mystery in God's formation of humankind. The breath of life from God upon contact with the lifeless body resulted in the creation of a living soul. We are not only body, we are also soul and spirit.

In this book, I will make references to concepts such as emotions, feelings, fears, etc. Laying this foundation is important to your understanding of these concepts as they relate to this book. In general, we are spirits with the ability to commune with God, who is also Spirit. We are also souls with an emotional nature. Additionally, we have bodies that carry out the dictates of the human spirit and soul. For example, when we feel hungry, we find something to eat. The body, soul, and spirit work in unity, which makes up the whole man. The purposes and plans we accomplish originate in our thinking and are manifested in our actions. This is where the concept of our mind takes shape. We have the ability to think, reason, and make decisions. The knowledge we receive ultimately influences our emotions and determines the actions we take with our bodies.

In this book, I will make references to the mind. In scripture, there are several meanings of the word. The general meanings from the Bible include, but are not limited to, the following: 1) imagination; 2) intellect; 3) thought; and 4) will. The goal of this guide is not to undertake an in-depth biblical study of the body, soul, spirit, and mind. Instead, it is simply to help the reader identify with the experiences that many people encounter in their quest to find peace or maintain peace in their lives. I hope to present a simple understanding of my experience without leaving the reader confused.

Living an overwhelming life of anxiety, fear, panic attacks, depression, oppression, distress, or any attack against the mind is a reality that some people struggle with every day. If you struggle with these things, you will find hope for a peaceful life in the pages of this book. You will come to realize that the peace of God that passes all your understanding is possible to obtain. God wants you to be free, indeed! I am writing this book around the time of Michael Jackson's, the "King of Pop," death. The news media has covered his life extensively. Much of what I have gained from the reports seems to indicate that his life was filled with fears, addictions, trauma, and several other unfortunate problems. Every individual will suffer trouble in this life. It is how we cope with trouble that determines our quality of life.

In 1996, I worked at a car dealership. While working one day, I sang one of my original songs, "See, But Don't Touch." The chorus was "See, see God inside me, no matter what Satan does, he can't touch me." One day later, I experienced a satanic attack of fear. Satan reminded me of a traumatic childhood experience of fear when I was locked inside a room. From that time, I wrestled with a more intense fear of being enclosed, commonly known as claustrophobia. Little did I know I would be tested and tried because of the words of a song I had written.

I realized that I did not overcome the childhood fear. On the day of the attack, every thought of being enclosed flooded my mind.

I focused on the thoughts constantly until they began to overtake me. The thoughts were so strong that I envisioned greater levels of the fear. Any area of enclosure caused fear to erupt in my mind. From my home to my car, I was crippled with fear. The devil was succeeding in engulfing me in constant fear. The fear was so crippling I remember staying in my bed without any hope of survival. Every day I was bombarded with tormenting thoughts. There seemed to be no way out and no way of deliverance. But, I still knew that God's Word was real and powerful. The only hope I had was what I knew God had done through his Word.

I cried for help every day. I could not sleep peacefully for months. The constant reminder of my fear was before me. This caused great distress in my everyday life. Even if I was able to fall asleep, I would be awakened by satanic nightmares, filled with fear. Most of my dreams were centered on my being enclosed in small spaces. My mind was consumed with fear, and I was slowly losing my spiritual foundation. One day, I was in my bed thinking on my hopelessness. I began to rest in my weakness and depend on God's strength. At that point, I heard a voice speaking softly from within me. I do not remember the exact words, but they were words of hope. I believe those words were "rise up." The words reminded me that God would deliver me, and they were the first glimpse of hope leading to my deliverance. From that day, I was empowered with special strength to begin to rise up from the bed of fear, torment, and defeat. I will never forget the scripture in the book of Psalms, which declared, "This poor man cried unto the Lord and the Lord heard him and delivered him from [ALL] his fears." I told myself, if God did it for the poor man, he can do it for me. From that day, I began to cry unto God for deliverance from fear.

During my experience, nobody's words consoled me. I was falling and falling with no one to help me. Almost everyone I spoke to had no idea what I was experiencing. Many of them only saw my experience as trivial. They had never heard of an attack of claustrophobia that rose to the level I was experiencing.

The truth of God's Word was the only weapon I had to survive the attacks. I knew that, based on the Bible, Faith and Love were my greatest weapons against claustrophobia, panic attacks, anxiety, etc. The Bible declares that perfect love casts out all fear. Also, I understood that faith is the opposite attribute of fear. From these basic truths, God began to reveal to me the remedies to deal with every form of emotional disorder. For one year, I meditated on the truths of God's Word every day. I studied the principles of his Word vigorously with one focus, deliverance from fear. My year-long ordeal left me with some precious insights about overcoming the battle against the mind. For the first time, I really began to understand what the Bible meant when it said, "I shall fear no evil."

In this book, I will share with you the truths God revealed to me in the Bible to help me deal with my fears. On a note of caution, if you do not believe in God and are not living a life pleasing to him in accordance to his Bible, these principles may be confusing to you.

1

The Battle of the Mind

When I joined the military, we trained in the field often. When we secured ourselves, we formed what is called a perimeter. The perimeter was usually shaped in a circle with an entrance point and several defense points located strategically around the perimeter. The purpose of the defense was to prevent infiltration of the perimeter and defend our position. We were reminded that, if we were infiltrated, the enemy could destroy us from within.

Knowing this, we guarded our post diligently day and night. The main control and every essential element of the military team were positioned inside the perimeter. From the main control, the strategies of attacks against the enemy were planned. To protect the perimeter, a code of entry was created every day and circulated to everyone throughout it. Anyone entering the perimeter, when challenged, was required to provide the code word. For example, the guard would say "black," and the soldier or individual seeking entrance would reply "cat." The codes were made up of two words. One was the challenge and the other was the response.

Even on the inside of the perimeter, the code words were used.

The objective was to keep the main control clear of any disruption. If the main control was dominated, the entire perimeter would be compromised, resulting in the defeat of the military team. In some instances, an intruder could infiltrate the perimeter.

Although this illustration does not capture the details of the attacks we face against our soul (emotional nature), I believe it provides a general idea of how important it is to guard our minds from intrusive and controlling thoughts. Once we have accepted Christ, he works to develop our defenses around our mind with his Word. When we study and understand the scriptures, the truth becomes our defense. Romans 12:2 declares, "Be not confirmed to this world: but be ye transformed by the renewing of your mind." We do this by testing every spirit who attempts to gain entrance into our lives. Evil spirits make suggestions to us in different ways. One way is through our thoughts. Negative thoughts should never be given the opportunity to dominate our thinking. We should never allow negative emotions to lead our thinking apart from the truth of God's Word. Even though negative thoughts such as fear and guilt may access our mind, we have to choose whether or not we will entertain them. The Bible directs us to cast down vain imaginations or thoughts from our mind.

The Word of God says that God will keep them in perfect peace whose mind is stayed upon him. A mind of perfect peace is not a battlefield. I do not believe it is God's will for us to be constantly fighting battles in our mind. The Bible declares that we should set our mind on honest, pure, just, and virtuous things. There should be no room for anything else. If we permit anything opposite of honesty, virtue, and praise to exist in our mind, we will begin to react negatively. We will become distressed, depressed, and oppressed. God has given us a sound mind. If we are constantly thinking on things of virtue and praise, we will leave no place for the devil.

As mentioned before, God taught us to cast down vain imaginations that exalt themselves in our minds against the knowledge of God. One preacher said we are to judge every thought or imagination coming to our mind and cast it down if it does not line up with God's peace. If it is an imagination of fear, cast it down before it can manifest itself in your actions. In the chapters to come, I will share some specific information to help you master your emotions and live a life free from worry, depression, fear, and oppression. My prayer is that the wisdom of these truths will help you to experience "the peace of God which passes all understanding."

2

Faith vs. Emotions

In essence, faith is believing the words and promises of God to be true and placing complete trust in God, knowing that he cannot lie. Faith is developed by hearing and practicing God's Word. During my times of despair, I noticed that my emotions wanted to be the leader of my life. I would react based on how I felt. Emotions are feelings that compel us to do things. Emotions are essential to our existence. We cannot deny them or live without them. However, we can control them by choosing to do God's will from the scriptures. God's Word in the book of Proverbs reveals that a man who can control his spirit is better than one who can capture a city. During my ordeal, if I felt fearful, anxious, or depressed, these feelings wanted to dominate me. This is why I developed the first principle, which I practiced in my despair: *Stay focused on righteousness; control your emotions by forcibly meditating on the Word of God.* The fact behind this truth is that Satan always bombards our mind with negative, suggestive thoughts in an effort to activate our thinking process. I used the word "forcibly" because the thoughts and feelings were so overpowering that, had I not forced myself to read the Bible, it would have seemed impossible. Under normal circumstances, reading the Bible was easy. I was known to read Bibles until the pages fell out. However, because of the fear, torment, and depression, I had no strength. It is okay to defy your feelings when they defy the truth and knowledge of God's Word. Even though I did not feel like reading the Bible, it was the right thing to do.

I knew that the best way to fight the fear was to develop my faith. The scripture states that faith comes by the hearing of God's Word. Your knowledge of God's Word will save you in times of trouble. Day by day, my faith was developing to the point where I could begin to feel better. The negative emotions were gradually losing their grip on me. The results were not seen overnight. I learned to take baby steps, which led to my ability to walk again. Faith without works is fruitless. According to Vernon Eng, one of my former Bible school teachers, "[our] faith is realized as strength in our circumstances, when we apply the truth. We have to work at it." The way to work our faith is to reestablish our actions with the Word of God. The reality is that sometimes this can take weeks, months, or even years, depending on the circumstances. When challenges are mounting, the temptation is to stop applying the truth of God's Word to our circumstances. What is important is that we never give up!

No matter how I tried to ignore the negative emotions, it seemed as if they were overpowering me. The devil tried to convince me that what I was experiencing was normal, but God's Word was saying something quite different. For example, "God has not given us the spirit of fear, but of power of love and of a sound mind." I actually thought this scripture was written by an alien because it seemed as if it was not working for me. I would tell myself there was no way I could have a sound mind. It was only after fighting hard for months to read the Bible in spite of how I felt that I was able to see that my emotions could not control me. I had the power to control my emotions! In essence, I had to learn to discipline my thought life. Unlike popular thought, if your mind is a constant battlefield, you are not living in peace. This is why it is very important to meditate on God's Word daily. Success in our thought life and ultimately our entire being depends on what we allow to dominate our minds.

I believe we cannot accept the lie that we must become infiltrated and overtaken by negative thoughts and emotions. God wants us to have the "mind of Christ." Christ was not defeated, fearful, and terrorized. He was and is the righteousness of God. Righteousness radiates from who he is. The book of Proverbs is accurate. A person is what he or she thinks.

A great philosopher, Rene Descartes, wrote, "I think, therefore I am." Hundreds of years before this, God revealed this truth in Proverbs. Jesus is the Righteousness of God because his thoughts are holy. What makes us what we are radiates from what we entertain in our minds. A person can only be what he or she thinks.

Certain emotions are formed from your thoughts. When you think on something, you will begin to feel and react to what you are thinking. After repetitious reactions to your emotions, you develop habits. When a habit is nurtured, a destiny is realized. If you are riding the elevator and everything is working mechanically, you can go from level to level without any interruptions. As soon as you hear an unfamiliar noise, you begin to think, *Something must be wrong.* When the elevator actually stops without opening, you begin to think about all that could have gone wrong. *What will happen now? Is there help on the way? Does anyone know the elevator is malfunctioning?* All these thoughts begin to come to the mind and trigger feelings of fear. You would achieve the opposite effect if you remained calm because you knew which buttons in the elevator to press for help. Instead of becoming fearful, you would be relaxed because you knew someone would respond to your call.

There must be discipline in our thoughts and a refusal to worry about things. The tendency to act in fear when unexpected things happen is normal. However, we can change our thinking and learn to be calm in trouble. Jesus was not too concerned when he was on the boat in the middle of a storm. Whenever trouble presented itself, he practiced being calm and collected.

As illustrated in the example using the elevator, thoughts of fear come from feelings of hopelessness. When we hear, see, or feel something, we begin to react. Depending on what we perceive, thoughts are produced. In spite of how you feel, you need to focus on what God says and live in hope in the midst of despair. The constant rehearsing of our thoughts acts on our emotional nature. From that point, we begin the process of becoming what we think.

The secret to a disciplined thought life is to dismiss the negative thoughts as soon as they come. If you rebuke the thoughts and replace them with thoughts of peace instead of fear, dismay, confusion, etc., you will walk in peace. Acting on your negative emotions will only take you on a roller-coaster ride in life.

3

Faith vs. Fear

In Chapter One, we discussed some general concepts of fear in relation to faith. In this chapter, we will discuss it in further detail. The concept of faith is opposite to the concept of fear. Fear operates when we believe a lie and put our trust in things that are false. Faith operates when we believe the truth and put our hope and trust in things that are true. The devil is a master of using fear to approach the gate of our minds. He may approach our mind with corrupt information that sometimes represents something that has not occurred and is usually filled with bad news. When we think on the information, we begin the process of activating the emotions of fear. An example of such a thought could be "What if the plane crashes on my flight?" Instead of rebuking the thought, you continue to think about all the bad news you've heard of plane crashes. Days before traveling, you hear about a plane crash and begin to relate the crash to your trip. On the day of your flight, you have an intense feeling of fear. While you are on the plane, all of a sudden, there is a drop in the altitude. You begin to scream in horror because you are acting on the negative thoughts.

Fear moves Satan, but faith moves God. Jesus would tell people that their faith made them free of sickness. The same is true for people who are constantly in fear of becoming sick; your doubt and fear can make you sick. Job said that the thing he feared the most came upon him.

Walking in fear cripples the body, soul, and spirit. You become easy prey for the devil when you are overwhelmed by thoughts of fear. Your decisions are all based on fear-filled thoughts. Your life is controlled by them. Many people are missing out on the joy of the Lord because they live in lies of fear that are constantly bombarding them. These lies can come from what others say about them or what they say about themselves. This is why we must remain focused on God's Word. The Bible reminds us to set our eyes on Jesus, "the author and finisher [perfector] of our faith." Judson Cornwell's early lesson, which sustained him more than sixty years in the ministry, came from that verse. He explained that when looking at Jesus, worship replaces worry, and adoration overcomes negative activity. "The upward gaze handles pride, fear, doubt and criticism."

To overcome claustrophobia I had to replace fearful thoughts with faith-filled thoughts. In order to do this, I had to apply every scripture in the Bible I could find about living a life free of fear. For almost one full year, I carried those scriptures with me on a daily basis and memorized as much of them as I could. The verses became a part of my thought process. Allow God's Word to become a part of your thought process. When you meditate on God's Words, you begin to act like God in any situation. God never reacts in fear to anything. Let your imaginations be of every good and Godly thing. The fruit of the Spirit is manifested when this is done. One of the fruits is peace. No wonder people of God who meditate on the Word of God prosper in everthing they do.

Below are some of the verses I used as spiritual vitamins to help me fight fear. The scriptures are quoted from the King James Version of the Bible:

Deuteronomy 31:6... Be strong and of good courage, fear not, nor be afraid of them: for the Lord thy God, he it is that doth go with thee; he will not fail thee, nor forsake thee.

1 John 4:17 and 18... Herein is our love made perfect, that we may have boldness in the day of judgment: because as he is, so are we in the world. There is no fear in love; but perfect love casteth out all fear; because fear has torment. He that feareth is not made perfect in love.

Psalm 46: 1-3... God is our refuge and strength, a very present help in trouble. Therefore will not we fear, though the earth be removed, and though the mountains be carried into the midst of the sea; Though the waters thereof roar and be troubled, though the mountains shake with the swelling thereof.

1 John 5:4... For whatsoever is born of God overcometh the world: and this is the victory that overcometh the world, even our faith.

Isaiah 41:10... Fear thou not; for I am with thee: be not dismayed, for I am your God: I will strengthen thee; yea, I will help thee; yea, I will uphold thee with the right hand of my righteousness.

Deuteronomy 20: 3 and 4... O Israel, ye approach this day unto battle against your enemies: let not your hearts faint, fear not, and do not tremble, neither be ye terrified, because of them. For the Lord your God is he that goeth with you, to fight for you against your enemies to save you.

Luke 12:4, 5, and 7… And I say unto you my friends, be not afraid of them that kill the body, and after that have no more that they can do. But I will forewarn you whom ye shall fear: fear him, which after he hath killed hath power to cast into hell; yea, I say unto you fear him. But even the very hairs of your head are all numbered. Fear not therefore: ye are of more value than many sparrows.

If you are stuck in the elevator, instead of thinking about what could go wrong, familiarize yourself with the buttons you need to press to get help and resist the thoughts of everything that can go wrong. Years after becoming victorious in the area of my emotions, I realized that the principles I learned in my distress strengthened me to the point where I could help someone else. If I had read a book similar to the one I am writing, I would have stopped the thoughts of fear from the door of my mind and fought with God's Word to cast down the evil imaginations.

A few years following my ordeal, I traveled to St. Louis, Missouri. I had the opportunity to go to the highest point located in the St. Louis Gateway Arch. If you have ever been there, you know that there is not much space in the arch. The move-around space is almost nonexistent on the climb in a very small cart lift. I was able to go to the top without any problems. Years after, I had an MRI and was enclosed for seventeen minutes in a very small opening. God replaced the fears with his faith. I learned that when I am with God and he is with me, there is no need to fear. Even if you walk through the valley of the shadow of death, you will fear no evil because God is King of the valley. He knows every turn. He created every valley. Who would you prefer to walk in the valley with? Again, I would say here, "God has not given you the spirit of fear, but of love, power, and a sound mind."

4

Always Stay Focused on God!

These words seem simple when we say them. But when last did you try to stay focused on God when you were facing certain calamity or even death? When there are obstacles everywhere, some people want to curse God rather than remain focused on him. The mind can easily be shifted from a focus on God to a focus on the situations and circumstances that come to us every day.

Constantly and consciously reject thought patterns that are contrary to perfect peace. Do not add negative thought to negative thought in your mind. Only think truth. Cast down the thoughts that make you feel depressed constantly. Add Godly thoughts to Godly thoughts instead.

I used the word "constantly" because there are times when day after day, month after month, I fought thoughts that would try to disrupt my peace. The devil knows to some extent the things that easily disturb you. It may be a boss who said something negative about you that constantly comes to your mind. You think about the remark every day until you become depressed. The devil will use the boss's remark to flood your mind until you begin to react negatively. The enemy will use your weaknesses to influence your destiny by creating a pattern of defeat in your thinking process. If you learn to reject the thought patterns that disrupt your peace, you will always be victorious in your thoughts.

Instead of developing a negative thought pattern, stay focused on God and think truthful things at all times. If the thoughts do not line up with God's Word, do not waste your time thinking on them. *To keep your mind focused, use the principle of God's Word in the book of Philippians, which teaches us to think on good, pure, just, and honest things.* I briefly shared this truth in Chapter One. Use this principle as a rule to govern your thinking, and your focus will be easier to maintain.

Remember that when you overcome in one area, the devil tries to destroy you in another area. Therefore, always stay focused on God, never allow anyone, anything, or any situation to lead you away from righteousness, and be aware that the devil will try every trick to deviate you from your focus of peace, joy, and total fulfillment in God.

I included the above nugget because sometimes you may feel that you have succeeded in applying the principles of this book, but all of a sudden, you may be attacked in a completely different area of your life. This may catch you off-guard and shake your faith. If you are not careful, you may even begin to doubt your stand in God and give in to the trial at hand. If you are aware of the tactics of the devil, you will know that he is an expert of disruption and trickery. The way to overcome the tricks of the enemy is to resist him. Rebuke his advances in Jesus' name, and he will flee from you.

5

Get Busy and Stay Busy for God

Living a healthy spiritual lifestyle is key to establishing healthy thoughts. The book of Proverbs reveals this secret. Proverbs 16:3 states, "[commit] thy works unto the Lord, and thy thoughts shall be established." It worked for me. When I am busy doing God's business, he orders my thinking. Have you ever noticed that when you do a particular thing repetitiously throughout the day, you dream about it when you are sleeping? We usually dream about things that affect us or become a part of our routine. Not only do we dream, but we think on them. When our thoughts are established, we become established as well. God directed us to renew our mind to prove the true acceptable and perfect will of God. The will of God is what we do. When we are purposefully doing it, our thoughts are directed by the Holy Spirit.

I have remained busy doing God's business. This has helped me to establish God's will. I have a purpose, a hope, and a dream. I have a reason to live to see another day. I get excited about my work for God. A good example is the writing of this book. I am also a song writer, musician, and a preacher. When I am occupied doing purposeful and meaningful things, my thoughts are focused and directed in God's purpose for me. This leaves less time for me to become occupied with fearful and foolish thoughts. This is important because if I were purposeless, I would have more time to devote my time to idle things.

Idle and purposeless involvement produces idle thoughts, which weaken the defense of your mind. In Chapter Three, I addressed the benefits of staying focused on God. The concept of committing your work to God is similar. My focus is maintained by my work. Staying busy in God's field of work has helped me to establish my thoughts. When I found the verse in the book of Proverbs, I wondered how in the world committing my work to God could help me control my thoughts. But, after studying the passage and applying it to my life, I realized the benefits. I believe this is why I am devoting this chapter to discussing this secret of God's Word. The verse is a practical passage of scripture. It calls for action on your behalf. It screams from the pages. Commit your work to God. Seek him for guidance, and he shall guide you with his will. Thoughts and ideas for God's ministry will flow to you like a river. You will conceive plans for new ministries. This is because you have tapped into God's vision for your life. The thoughts that will flood your mind will be inspired by the Holy Ghost.

6

Forget Yesterday's Old Thoughts: "Celebrate Today!"

Yesterday's old thoughts will fade away when you learn to take a moment at a time. Jesus said, take no thought for certain things because sufficient is the evil of one day.

God has empowered the soul to heal itself, similar to how the body recovers from scars and wounds. If you were wounded, you would dress the wound and, as time progressed, it would heal. If you constantly remove the dressing and open the wound, it will hamper the healing process. Eventually, the wound may become infected and you may have other complications.

God's Word instructs us to cast our cares upon him. In other words, we should never have a need to be worrying about anything. Worry is the devil's way of feeding our thoughts and disrupting our emotional nature. Give God your cares and leave them with him. Let God think on your cares for you. Let him figure out the details of your trials. He is more than qualified to fix problems.

I am also referring to situations that were already resolved. In my experience, there were times when I overcame a particular attack, but the devil would bring the same old thoughts to me. The same claustrophobic attacks would try to bombard me again. Sometimes I would get caught up in the same defeating thoughts for days. Eventually, the feelings of fear would take hold again. Interestingly, this repeated cycle only made me stronger. From this, I phrased the aforementioned italicized statement to remind myself what to do when old thoughts came back. I would practice this over and over again until it became a part of me.

I believe this was because God enabled me to conquer the defeating thoughts. I knew for a fact that if I would constantly reject foolish thoughts that produced fear and depression, they would eventually fade away. For years I practiced this concept. I also learned not to worry by taking a moment at a time. Jesus expressed this concept in the book of Matthew in his teaching against worry. Jesus' revelation that we take "no thought" for certain things is important because he was teaching us the secret of overcoming worry. He was showing us how to protect ourselves from old, unresolved issues. He was teaching that we should not worry about what we will need to wear, eat, etc. Jesus explained that he already made provision for his people. As such, we had no need to worry.

Since God has already delivered you from the battle inside your mind, why do you want to continue fighting in your head? Why not give God your concerns? You have enough to deal with on a daily basis. So, take a moment at a time and "chill." Take "no thought." If you do this, you will have a happier, peaceful, and fruitful day.

I will never forget the lesson God taught me in July 2010 about the importance of taking one day at a time. I read an article that was featured in the *Men's Fitness* magazine called "Today Is Not Tomorrow." The article addressed the idea that we should be careful not to find ourselves thinking about tomorrow. Today's challenges are enough. Taking baby steps is important, even when we are not seeing, feeling, or experiencing full freedom from our challenges. I came across this information about two days after writing an exhortation to myself entitled "Today." About one week after this, my family took a trip to Disney World in Orlando, Florida. I quickly noticed that on every receipt in my pocket there was a theme that simply read, "Celebrate Today." I was concerned at that point that God was speaking to me directly. He wanted me to learn that, in the midst of my many challenges, I only needed to cast them on him and prepare to have a party every day. The night after I noticed the receipt, I shared it with my mother-in-law, who was on the trip with us. As soon as I told her this, she walked into her room in the suite we were sharing, and Joel Osteen was preaching a message about God's grace to empower us on a daily basis. The entire message focused on living one day at a time. He stated that God only gives us the grace for today. His mercies are new every single morning. We don't need to think ahead and worry, not even about the next minute, hour, or six hours. He will give us the ticket to ride the day in the morning; we only need to give it back to him, and he will drive us through the day. Don't worry about the journey, only board the train and begin the journey. By this time, I was almost freaked out. However, I was not surprised because I know how God speaks to his people.

The next day, I went to the mall with my wife. She called me to a store to buy a pair of comfort shoes. When I walked in the store, I started examining the shoes. While doing so, I heard a song being played in the store. The singer continued singing without stopping, "Celebrate Today, Celebrate Today, Celebrate Today…!" I called the attendant quickly and asked her who was singing the song, but she was unable to give me any information. After those two weeks of revelation from God, I was convinced. I quickly decided to engrave my experience in my life.

A couple of weeks after the experience, I preached a message entitled "Today Is Not Tomorrow: Celebrate Today." *Men's Fitness* magazine and Disney Land are secular establishments. Yet, they have learned the truth Jesus was teaching over two thousand years ago. I was fascinated. I have since learned that, just as we need daily food to remain physically strong, we need God's daily Word to stay spiritually strong. The Bible teaches us how to pray by guiding us to pray, "Give us this day our daily bread." Daniel prayed three times a day. Sometimes in our experience of hurt and emotional distress, we feel as if we cannot make it through the day. Many of us have contemplated suicide. We feel we just can't make it, and we do not have the strength to face our dilemmas. Do not believe those lies! The devil knows that if you pray even for ten minutes, you will have the strength to make it. He deceives you into thinking that you can't make it. Do not listen to him! Rebuke him and get down on your knees. Jesus, in the garden where he prayed just before he was arrested, prayed hard. The Bible says that while he prayed, an angel strengthened him.

Daniel prayed frequently. His prayers were pivotal to his ability to survive a lion's den. He always prayed when he was faced with difficult circumstances. However, his prayers did not begin when the problem came. He prayed every day, in the good times and in the challenging times. Jesus said pray that you are strong when the temptation comes. Your prayer is the funnel God uses to pour himself in the tank of your spirit. Even though God is already residing in us, we still need to communicate with him.

Enjoy your day! Spend time with God, but also include time with family and friends. Some personal practical ways I dominated the recurring and discouraging thoughts that were undermining my thought process are as follows: 1) playing pool; 2) taking a vacation; 3) reading a good book; 4) watching an inspiring movie; 5) listening to Godly music; 6) walking on the beach; and 7) playing my favorite sport. Whatever good and pure fun that takes your mind off the clutter of life, go for it! You may not do what I did, but I can assure you that these things were very essential to my balance. Find ways to celebrate each day with good, holy, fun things.

7

The True Power of Peace

Jesus is the agent who has given us true peace. He is also known as the "Prince of Peace." It is important for us to understand that the power is not ours. We cannot overpower the enemy without the power of Jesus. God's Word reveals that we are to be strong in the Lord and in the power of his might. The truth about peace is that when we seek God's presence in worship, he fills us with the power of his might. What is interesting about this truth is that we cannot generate the strength of ourselves. God is our strength. He is our strength to overcome any obstacle, weakness, situation, or circumstance. When Jesus died and rose again, he rose with the keys to all our needs. This includes freedom from all the works of the devil. Because of his work on the cross, we have access to the power in his name. When we cast down imaginations, we do it in the name of Jesus.

There were times that thoughts were trying to flood my mind like a broken pipe. No matter how hard I tried to avoid the thoughts, they would continually bombard me. At that point, I cast them down in the name of Jesus. I rebuked them and called on the name of Jesus. The power of God set me free the same hour. I experienced supernatural deliverance from those thoughts. The devil knows that if he can control your thinking, he can control you. He is aware that the way to win you is to win your thinking. He is aware that if he can produce false evidences appearing real in your mind, he can get you to react in fear. He is the master of lies and illusion. He will do everything in his power to attack you, especially when you are doing God's Kingdom business. To win the battle against our minds, we must use the name of Jesus. We have to realize that the power in his name is available every minute.

Wherever the disruption of your peace entered, God can remove it. In the book of Psalms, a man cried to the Lord, and he delivered him from all his fears and troubles. The fact is this: God can and will completely deliver you from your childhood trauma. He can sever you completely. He can heal you to the point where he reverses your knowledge and gives you a new perspective on your past failures and weaknesses. Paul said he forgot things that were in the past and pressed forward to the mark of the high calling in Christ Jesus. God himself cast our sins in the sea of forgetfulness. I have learned to forget the fears of the past that were produced by sin. I traded my fear for the faith of the Lord. I severed ties with the past weaknesses of the flesh, and I am focusing every day on a new life in Christ Jesus. I have released myself from the bondages of my past through the acceptance of the blood of Jesus. We have to come to the place where we only know what it means to be free.

8

Making Sense of Peace

In the presentation of the past seven chapters, I hope you have grasped an idea of how God can energize you to live an overcoming life in Christ. The peace of God passes all the understanding of our carnal, earthly senses. I live each day because God is in me. When fears, doubt, and anxiety come against my mind, I have a choice to lend my thinking to them. Even if I am overcome for a time by these emotions, God has promised he will never leave me nor forsake me. He gives me the strength to overcome them and reminds me of his Word. Without God, I can do nothing. The peace of God, which passes all understanding, is real and attainable. The secret to obtaining the peace of God is simply accepting the work of his son on the cross of Calvary. When we receive him in our hearts and begin to walk a life pleasing to him, we are guaranteed the promise of peace every single moment of our lives!

The scripture is clear. God will keep us in perfect peace when our mind is focused on him. Making sense of this may seem hard at times. How can God keep me in perfect peace when my mind is on him? You may have tried doing this over and over again, and you are still tormented. I experienced the same thing in my ordeals. I would concentrate on God in the moment, hoping peace would come that minute. God's peace is always present. Sometimes we go through circumstances that alter our peace of mind. However, I believe the verse works when we are actively walking in God's will by renewing our mind on a daily basis. In Chapter Five I discussed getting busy for God. The Word of God is written on a page, but the results of the Word are realized in our actions.

If you want to experience the true peace beyond your ability to comprehend, follow the nuggets of truth in this book that were revealed to me in my times of trouble. God allows us to go through trials to help others. It is not a coincidence that you are reading this book. You were destined to read it. Your life will never be the same again! You will rise up and live! Your emotions will not control you any longer. Fear will not dominate your thoughts. You will be free from defeat in Jesus' name. I declare that you are completely delivered from the battle that is constantly raging in your mind. You are at peace in your body, soul, and spirit, and only thoughts of virtue and praise are exalted in your life.

It is very important to note that the principles in this book can work, not only with dealing with fearful thoughts, but with everyday thoughts that come to your mind and are uncomfortable and unwelcomed. I have used these same principles when I encounter a situation that challenges me to be angry, mad, sad, resentful, etc. It is also very important for you to know that many actions begin with a thought. Some actions are premeditated, while others may be spontaneous, but a high percentage of our actions begin with a thought. This is a scriptural concept. The Bible shares with us that we speak only what is in our hearts, and we become only what we think. There are people who try to intimidate you with their words. If you replay the words in your mind and welcome them continually into your thought process, you can become resentful and hateful. It is not unhealthy to address intimidation by others, but, once the problem is addressed, it should remain settled. Pray for the person and leave it there. Further thoughts will lead to more thoughts and only give the devil an opening to produce unhealthy emotions in you. Much of what is allowed to form your character comes from your power to choose what to think.

Temptations

The temptation to be unfaithful to your wife or husband can also be conquered by your will to follow God's Word. But how is this accomplished in the thought process? First, temptation presents itself through the senses, but you have the power to challenge the temptation. Simply using the method of positive thinking may not be enough. Some good books were written about the power of our thoughts, but, without the application of God's Word, there is limited power in positive thinking. When the thoughts to be unfaithful come to your mind, you must cast them down and replace the imaginations with the truth of God's Word.

God's Word declares that we should not covet someone else's spouse. Also, it is clear that we should not look at the opposite sex lustfully or we commit adultery in our hearts. Jesus said we commit adultery without the act by simply entertaining the thought. If the thought comes to you, it does not mean you have sinned. This means that you have been tempted. You have sinned when you are tempted and you intentionally carry out the act in your heart, rather than casting down the imagination. The concept here is simple. Dismiss the thought of lust when it comes. Rebuke it with God's Word and remain focus on living right. This can be easier said than done. What is important is that you not give in to the sinful advances of the opposite sex.

The temptation to steal, cheat, and commit fraud can be overcome by the same process. The victory depends on you. If you are enticed and, because of your lust for things, entertain the thoughts to commit sinful acts, you will. Now, there are consequences of your actions. You may not be emotionally disturbed by your actions until you find yourself in a divorce proceeding or other unfortunate circumstance.

Conflicts

I also use the principles in my book to generally deal with others, confront situations, resolve conflict, etc. I will talk a little about resolving conflicts. Today many people harbor resentment and unforgiveness in their hearts because of conflicts on the job, on the street, or in their homes. When we are involved in conflicts, we are also required to be disciplined in our thinking. Solomon said a "soft answer" turns away wrath, but soft answers only come from people with controlled thoughts. Soft answers are not heated and filled with resentment and hate. In conflicts, your mind is stormed with what you can do to someone else who has hurt you. Day after day, night after night, month after month, you may think about what you can do or how you can get even. The result is someone who is emotionally scarred by what people did to them. They always make excuses for why they will never forgive others or why they need to get even. The opposite is true for people who replace the negative thoughts produced from conflict with peaceful ones. They are always looking for a way to keep the peace and offer forgiveness. The key to success is the Word of God. Again, I repeat the same lesson. If there is no scripture in you to counteract the negative thought, it is hard to avoid thinking on the wrong thing.

Always rebuke the negative thoughts and remind yourself of the proper way to treat others based on God's Word. It reinforces the principle that peace should always be maintained in your mind with God's words of defense. Jesus did this when the devil tempted him. Jesus counteracted all of Satan's advancements with the scripture verse pertaining to the attack. He did not take one moment to ponder or consider the kingdoms Satan promised him if he would cast himself down. Had he allowed the thoughts to enter his mind and he continued the thought process and accepted the offer, he would have been conquered. In the end, he revealed the source of his strength against Satan's mind attacks: "Man shall not live by bread alone, but by every word which proceeds out of the mouth of God." This is what I have reinforced in these practical ways to make sense of peace. Peace can only be mastered by the Master, Jesus Christ himself. He overcame the devil so that the power of his Word could protect our peace of mind. That is why the Bible says we should let the mind of Christ be in us. His mind is the Master of our mind. Since this is the case, it is impossible for the devil to overcome us, except when we permit him.

Overcoming temptations and conflicts are only two ways to make sense of living in peace. However, the principles of God's Word when it pertains to the peace of your soul, spirit, and body can be applied to any situation you may face. The core of peace rests in the transformation of our entire being. God's supernatural peace is funneled into our being by God's Word. Having faith in what God says is the key. Refocus on the scriptures presented in this book on peace. Since God wrote the concepts, they are true. The question is…whether we believe them or not.

Here is my guiding principle to maintaining a peaceful life (as I shared in Chapter Six). I begin my day with this scripture: "This is the day that the Lord has made, I will rejoice and be glad in it." Notice God made the day for us. If we go back to Genesis, when God created everything, he called his creation "good." What is also important to note about this verse is the word "will." I will rejoice and be glad. There is nothing hidden in the verse. God is simply saying since he made the day, you can choose to rejoice and be glad in it.

We usually say that happiness is a choice. Well, we are right. The only problem is the process. The day may begin well, but challenges can happen in an instant—you may learn you have cancer, your mother has died, your money was lost in the stock market, etc. Obviously, if your loving mother dies, you will not be going around laughing and having a good time. Solomon said there is a time to laugh and a time to cry. The Bible promotes balance. A time of grief is healthy but, if not kept in check, can grow into depression and ultimately have other negative emotional impacts. Naturally going through events that warrant your emotional responses does not mean that you have lost your joy. However, there must be a balance to maintain your joy in the Lord. What you allow to dominate your thought process and infiltrate your mind ultimately reaches your will. How will you handle the cancer?

How will it affect your day? You answer for yourself. If all the challenging things happen, how can you rejoice and be glad? I believe that the answer is in your will. What "will" you do?

From the challenges I have experienced in my many years on earth, I coined this phrase, "My worst days are my best days." I know that trouble comes to make me stronger. If this is the case, why would I be disappointed with becoming stronger? Instead, I should be disappointed if I am growing weaker. It goes back to God's Word again. Depending on what happens in my day, I know I have to apply God's Words to my thoughts to reject negative ones. I do not look for bad things to happen in any given day. If a challenge comes, I confront it with all the principles God taught me. In the end, I am not too disturbed at all. I make sure that whatever things are honest, pure, just, holy, and sensible fill my mind. Anything else, I cast down quickly. The promise from God's Word is that the peace of God, which passes all understanding, will keep my heart and mind. It works all the time. If it seems as if it is not working for you, keep working at it. Become a Bible student instead of a Bible reader, and pray without ceasing.

I explained several scenarios to deal with negative thoughts and to maintain your peace. If you apply them to your life, you will not only enjoy today, but even greater, you will enjoy every day. You will take control of your future. The Bible will become the measuring stick of your self-worth, peace, and joy. No longer will you be subject to every whim of your emotions. You will form the emotions that are healthy by what you allow to enter your mind and ultimately your spirit. You will have peace beyond your own understanding.

If you read this book but you do not have the power of God to confront the negative things happening to you, pray this prayer with me. "Father, you sent your son, Jesus Christ, to die in my place. He purchased me with the blood he shed on the cross. I believe and confess with my mouth that he is Lord. Save me from this day forward in Jesus' name!"

www.ingramcontent.com/pod-product-compliance
Lightning Source LLC
Chambersburg PA
CBHW031333290526
45784CB00014B/2642